Butterfly Soup

A Guide to
Changing Your Life
(from the inside out)

by

Aurora J. Miller

Butterfly Soup: a guide to changing your
    life (from the inside out)
© 2017 Aurora J. Miller

 *Butterfly Soup Media*
is an imprint of Portal Center Press, LLC

www.portalcenterpress.com

ISBN: 978-1-936902-25-5

printed in USA

For more support and guidance on working through the transformation process,
go to: www.Butterfly-Soup.com

This book is dedicated to you,
a seeker of change
who can transform the world
by transforming yourself

Contents

INTRODUCTION

How many times have you set a goal but given up before you accomplished it?

Or put off reaching for something that you really wanted because it was too hard, or you couldn't figure out where to begin? Decided to change your lifestyle, to be more healthy and more productive, but then couldn't sustain it and reverted to your old outdated way of being?

It's not your fault if you've struggled to make positive, lasting changes in your life. If you don't understand how the transformation process works, how can you be expected to implement it reliably or consistently?

So instead most of us wander through life, making half-hearted attempts to be better, to find happiness, but mostly succumbing to numbing the pain we feel because there don't seem to be any other real options.

But it doesn't have to be this way. You *can* transform yourself. You can set the most outrageous, outstanding goal for yourself, and achieve it. You can allow yourself to yearn for your heart's desire, knowing that you have the tools to get from where you are now to where you're living your dream.

The transformative process outlined in these pages will help you understand the nature of change, and how to implement it. It will prepare you for the resistance that invariably rises, which is where most of us get frustrated and give up. And it will help you begin to identify the stories you tell yourself about yourself, about the world, and about how other people see you so that you can be more effective in every aspect of your life.

One of the most insidious is our "looking good story," which we tell every day without even realizing it. This story tells the people around us that we are competent, capable, effective, friendly, all sorts of positive things. That we "look good". We conceal aspects about ourselves that don't support this story, and we try to show up in ways that aren't authentic if it serves the purpose.

Laid out like that it sounds bad, but it actually served an evolutionary function: When humans lived in tribes scattered across the planet, it was essential that we be accepted, or else we might be turned away from the community, which would basically have been a death warrant. That acceptance-seeking trait has been handed down through the generations, and continues to be a subconscious need for us.

Meanwhile it's been reinforced through the media that we have to fit in to be okay. That we have to conform to someone else's ideal. That happiness is attainable only when we look and spend like movie stars or perfect Pinterest parents. That personal authenticity, being true to ourselves regardless of how it looks on the outside, is abnormal or even deviant. Every day in advertisements and television shows and movies and news programs we see evidence which supports the importance of maintaining the "looking good story" facade.

But when we realize the impact that maintaining this story has had, the way it has drained us, we can begin to make different choices. We can choose happiness, and allow our community to see us and love us as our true authentic selves.

A wise woman once told me, "Your body always knows the truth." Actually she said it more than once, because I had a hard time getting it. Yet we all talk about it all the time. From being weak in the knees to being aflame with passion, our emotions are reflected in our physical experience. Certainly when thinking about things we don't want, or what we desperately do want, our bodies respond accordingly. If we pay attention, our bodies will tell us the difference between truth and story, and we can use that truth as a compass to guide us through the transformation.

Like the caterpillar that literally dissolves into a "soup" as part of its metamorphosis to a butterfly, you may find that this process changes you deeply, and irrevocably. You may find brand new stories to tell about yourself, and begin to experience life with a sense of wonder and excitement that you never thought possible.

The format you'll find here is akin to a computer manual, designed to get you quickly up to speed then out in the world to implement what you've learned, complete with a Troubleshooting section at the back which resolves the most common problems people run into when trying to affect change.

If you're anything like me you have a stack of self-help and healing books gathering dust, each with a couple of dog-eared pages to go back and reference later; my hope is that this content is so succinct and useful that every page would need to be dog-eared. That you'll keep this book handy as a reference to help guide you through life's many challenges.

Because the thing is, we're never done changing. We are constantly evolving and adapting, setting goals large and small, meeting resistance, and overcoming or succumbing. We are regularly confronted with choices to make that define us, that set or change our trajectory. Sometimes we're making several changes or pursuing multiple goals simultaneously, and each one is at a different stage in the process. But ultimately the process is always the same.

So take a deep breath, and think about the you you've longed to be. Then read on, and learn how to make that vision a reality!

Stage 1: Precipitate of Change

The caterpillar's transition begins when its bulk has exceeded its skin, as anyone who's read *The Hungry Caterpillar* can attest. Similarly, many of us seek change when we've outgrown the situation in which we've been living. Sometimes there's nothing wrong per se, but we have the sense that there's something more for us out there, or something doesn't feel right. Maybe we realize we've been in a position of stasis for too long, and we need some kind of change in our lives. Sometimes there are alarm bells because our system is on the verge of breakdown.

This is the "a-ha" moment, the realization that something's got to give. Some shift in awareness happens that causes us to seek an alternate way of being. It may be as sudden as lightning bolt, or slowly dawn over a long period of time. One way or another, a season of change has begun.

You are not alone.

We all know this is a time of great change. Technology is making advances almost faster than we can keep up with. Weather patterns are shifting all over the world. Marginalized groups are standing up and demanding to be heard. And many of us are beginning to heed the call of our inner voices to do more, to be more, than we thought we were capable of.

Meanwhile the Baby Boomers are moving into retirement, in many cases with more energy and more resources than any previous generation, so have an opportunity to redefine what retirement looks like. Millennials are beginning to move into positions of economic and political power, and bring with them a set of expectations and ideals that will no doubt force an evolution in the institutions to which they turn their attention.

Gen-X'ers, the latch-key generation which for years has felt like an afterthought at best while shuttled between broken households and later broken companies, frantically trying to piece together a livelihood out of the crumbs they've been offered, continue to try to figure out where they fit. How they can make a difference with what resources they do have.

Another big shift that may be applicable has been identified and defined by astrologers: The Age of Pisces is moving into the Age of Aquarius. Potentially dubious science, yet we can see evidence to support it. Pisces was focused on rigid, established models of religion, where Aquarius focuses more on inner truth. Similarly, science is less dogmatic, less captive to hard rules, and more a process of intuitive exploration. Some say that the emergence of quantum physics and the quantifying of metaphysics are indicators of this transition between Ages.

It's also been suggested that the Age of Aquarius promises a breakdown of gender roles and binary identities, as well as class structure. Regardless of whether one buys into the notion of Astrology, we can certainly see these shifts on the news and in our communities.

We're also seeing big changes in the institutions that were created to serve us. Political systems that were supposed to have sufficient checks and balances to prevent oligarchs from taking power and from being tied to the purse strings of corporations. Financial systems that were supposed to safeguard our resources, now often bleeding us dry. Industry that was designed to make our lives easier, both in the workplace and at

home, now implementing "planned obso-
lescence" and other similar offenses that
make our lives more frustrating and difficult.

All of this is to say that if you're feeling like it's time to make a significant
change in your life or your community,
you're certainly not alone. You are joined
by the bulk of humanity all over the
planet, people who re-cognize that the
status quo no longer serves us.

The Nature of Change

Some try to argue that on the whole,
change isn't necessary. That if everything's working more or less, things
should stay as they are. "If it ain't broke,
don't fix it." "The devil you know is safer
than the devil you don't."

But the world doesn't work that
way. Rivers change directions, albeit
slowly, as they erode rock and move sed-
iment. Continents drift as the plates on
which they rest are pulled by the Earth's

ever-rotating core. Even the magnetic poles are moving!

On a less geologic, more personal level, we ourselves are changing every single day as a result of the ideas and experiences to which we are exposed. Those who resist change become more calcified in their thoughts and beliefs, which itself is a change of sorts. Just the process of aging, of moving "from dust to dust" as it were, evokes a dramatic shift as we transition between developmental stages.

If you think about how the world looked to you when you were young, compared to how it looks now, you will likely see a significant difference. Many of us as children hardly have a sense that the world exists beyond our own neighborhood or town. We may have known the names of far off places like France or Zanzibar or Hong Kong, but they were as mythical as Atlantis or

Camelot until we had a framework that could make sense of them.

Developmentally, that's a normative experience. We need a framework to be able to "know" the truth of something. It's no different with conscious, intentional, personal change. Without a framework, or at least a set of guideposts to follow, it's difficult to affect the changes we seek to make.

Nature handles change in a variety of ways, but the ones most of us are familiar with are evolution and adaptation. In elementary school we learned that Man is descended from monkeys, as a result of something called Natural Selection. Maybe later on we learned a little more about how Natural Selection works, "survival of the fittest," that those who adapted in ways that were more effective at dealing with life's problems were more likely to procreate (have children), and pass on those successful adaptations to their offspring who in turn were more likely to be successful and procreate.

A study that I always found fascinating concerned grey moths in London. In the 1800s during the peak of coal pollution, houses and trees were coated in a dark dust, so the population of moths as a whole grew darker, because they were more effectively camouflaged. Lighter moths, which stood out against the dark surfaces, were more likely to be picked off and eaten by birds before they had an opportunity to procreate. Then in the mid-20th century when less coal was being used, the population of moths were lighter in color—because now the lighter moths had the more effective camouflage, against the less coal-covered surfaces.

Evolution and adaptation are more nuanced than huge changes that take eons to show up. They can also be subtle changes that ebb and flow according to the influences in the world around them.

As humans, we've become disconnected from the biological imperative of adaptation with regard to our ecological niche. Instead we've taken to adapting the world around us to fit our whims. Which is effective up to a point on the physical level, but doesn't work so well on personal and interpersonal levels.

If we use that study about the grey moth as a metaphor for our human, interpersonal experience, there is an opportunity to look at a number of ways in which we each adapt to different environments, as we go through life. We adopt new slang or local idioms when we interact with different groups of people. We dress differently for some jobs than others. We naturally, often subconsciously, adapt to the changing world around us as a way to improve our chances at success.

In relationships, we are particularly prone to adapting. What works with one person, makes them feel heard and cared for, often doesn't work with another person. Gary Chapman in his book *Love Languages,* points out some of the different ways people communicate their wants and needs, and suggests that if we can adapt our ways of interacting to include those that the other person finds meaningful, the "language they are fluent in," then our relationships are more likely to flourish and thrive.

Some of us tend to adapt to relationships in a way that can be counterproductive, such that we squelch pieces of ourselves for the happiness of the other. Again, adaptation is a means to success, but in such cases we have to ask ourselves what does success look like? If we're not being authentic, not embodying our whole and true selves, can a relationship truly be successful?

If we're able to move the adaptive process from the subconscious to the mindful, to consciously look for opportunities to change the ways in which we show up in the world, those innate skills and tendencies can support us in experiencing the success we seek.

If we see change not as something to be feared, but rather a natural function of the living world of which we are a part, then we are free to embrace the journey to our heart's desire. We can allow the process of transformation to begin, and move into a place where we can embody our dreams.

Change in Western Culture

Every generation for the last several centuries has tried to affect change in one way or another. From the sexual revolution and the Civil Rights movement in the '60s and '70s, back to the '30s and '40s with the rise of modern infrastructure, back to the Suffragette movement and Prohibition, and further back to pioneers, explorers, and revolutionaries. As each generation felt stifled by the status quo, they set out to make significant shifts for themselves and for their communities.

There has also been resistance to those changes. Sort of a cultural inertia that encourages people to say, "This is how it's always been, there's no reason to change it now."

But just as Newton's First Law states, "An object at rest tends to stay at rest," the reverse is also true: Once movement begins, an object tends to keep moving. So even though there will always be resistance to change, change will also always be an inevitability.

We'll get more into the immediate, personal experiences of resistance in stage 4, but from a broad strokes cultural perspective, a lot of the resistance we're seeing right now in terms of legislation being rolled back and the renewal of conservative thinking is actually a quite natural response to the social and economic changes that have been taking place over the last 50 years.

Because form resists change, and cultural or national identity is a form, it is to be expected that there will be a degree of pulling back on the reins to offset any significant shifts. And yet, the inevitability of momentum ensures the progress in spite of the backlash.

It's interesting that in this nation built by pioneers, by industrialists and inventors, we have become a country that is resistant to adopting new ideas and new ways of being. That rather than continuing to be on the forefront of technological and environmental development, we remain economically focused on the old days of coal and oil.

That in a country home to multiple sexual revolutions, we still find ourselves beholden to the Puritanical morés of the original colonists, discouraged from blazing our own trails and forging our own unique identities.

James Baldwin, a champion of the Civil Rights movement, said "Not everything that is faced can be changed, but nothing can be changed until it is faced." In our communities and our personal lives, we need to face the truth that we see around us before we can affect any real change.

We need to be honest with ourselves in ways that can feel uncomfortable, and sometimes scary, so that we can identify the changes that need to be made. Then we can set about making those changes, and use the principle of momentum to continue them to completion.

"The Center Will Not Hold"

The need for change can show up in a number of different ways, ranging from a mild inclination to try something new, to a driving desperate need reminiscent of Yeats' poem *The Second Coming* quoted above. What they all have in common is an awareness that some deep need isn't being met. Some hole exists that needs to be filled.

Whether it's a new job, a new hobby, a new love, a new way of being in the world, the realization of a lifelong dream that can't be ignored any longer, things simply *cannot* continue as they have been.

Many of us disregard the early stages of this awareness, because we don't have time to dig into something new, or we have a subtle but powerful fear of the unknown, or because we honestly feel trapped where we are and the idea of something different seems impractical if not out and out impossible.

Yet when ignored, this need can induce symptoms of depression and/or anxiety, as the nervous system becomes overwhelmed by the strain of trying to maintain an inauthentic way of being. Often reported by women in their 30s and 40s who have spent years focusing on the needs and desires of others without managing their own self care, continued disregard of these symptoms can easily result in adrenal burnout and even physical collapse.

It's also totally normative to feel anger or grief in this stage, particularly when we feel we're "not ready" to make a change. Letting go of old ways of being, of old plans or relationships that no longer serve us can be really difficult. But if we harness the winds of change and allow them to propel us into stage 2, rather than staying stuck in the grief, then the real fun can begin.

Ideally, stage 1 is a time of excitement, to find out what the future holds. To embrace the old pioneering spirit, and prepare for a journey to meet your authentic self and embody your heart's desire!

These case studies are fictionalized versions of real people, to help you see the transformative process in action.

CASE STUDY: Jane, stage 1

Jane was living the life she had always seen for herself: married with two wonderful kids, and a job that (for the most part) met her family's needs. Though like most Americans she and her husband worried about money, Jane recognized that they were incredibly fortunate to have the comfort and security they enjoyed.

And yet, Jane was miserable. And she didn't know why.

Most of the time she ignored the feeling, because she didn't have time to be present to it. Her days were filled with paperwork and house-work, kissing skinned knees and last minute trips to the grocery store; with her mind jam-packed with all the things she had to remember, there wasn't room for the things she was trying to for-get.

But then her eye would fall on that stain in the corner of the living room floor, that she nev-er found time to clean and her husband never seemed to notice. Or she'd be wracked with guilt when she prioritized her job's needs over her children's—or her children's needs over her job's. Or she'd take an extra second at the bathroom mirror and really look at herself, and see that she wasn't as "sexy" as she once was. And then she'd criticize herself for being so vain, for not feeling gratitude for everything she *did* have, and she'd try to get on with her day.

She knew she wasn't the only one, all her friends said the same, but none of them had any answers either. So they drowned their woes in wine, consoling themselves that they were at least better than some of the other moms they knew, and secretly prayed things would get easier. Somehow.

But then one night while Jane was folding the kids' laundry, tears started streaming down her face. She curled up on the floor surrounded by the always-insurmountable piles of clean and dirty clothes and sobbed uncontrollably.

Jane had realized that she had worked herself to exhaustion, and everything she did was for somebody else. Not a single part of her life was for her own happiness and wellbeing. And she just couldn't live that way anymore.

CASE STUDY: Shea, stage 1

Shea was a non-binary person (who used they/them pronouns instead of he/him or she/her) who worried a lot about the future. It seemed like everywhere they looked were signs of collapse, of destruction, and Shea felt completely overwhelmed.

What action could any one person take to make any kind of a difference, when the ice caps are melting and the bees are dying, and there is so much senseless violence happening all over the world?

Having always thought of themself as a seeker for truth, Shea turned to spiritual doctrines for comfort and solace, but found none. They were all written so long ago, that even though the wisdom was universal the practical applications were not.

And yet, Shea knew they couldn't just stay in bed and pull the covers over their head, much as they might like to. Somehow they had to find something, anything to do, that could feel like it made a difference. However small. Somehow they had to find a way to take their power back.

How to recognize it:
- ➢ Unexplained irritability
- ➢ Lassitude
- ➢ Excessive boredom
- ➢ Overconsumption (of food, drink, media, etc.)
- ➢ Depression / Anxiety

Action steps:
- ✓ Listen to the messages your body is sending you
- ✓ Look around for the cause, the aspect of your life that needs to change
- ✓ Begin to strengthen and follow your inner compass, which points towards

your happiness (more on this in stage 2)

Stage 2: Building the Chrysalis

In another modality, this stage might be identified as the crucible, the mechanism that generates and facilitates change. The caterpillar builds the chrysalis to protect it during its metamorphosis, but also to bring its imaginal cells out of dormancy so they can create the framework for the butterfly that will follow. For us, this is a time to collect data and tools, develop a support system, set a trajectory, and create the plan that will manifest as our own metamorphosis.

It's OK Not to Know the Specifics

It can feel really frustrating to know that you want something different, but not know exactly what that is. How can you make a plan if you don't know where you're going? It's easy to fall into a pattern where you're spinning and spinning, looking for something, *anything* that promises relief from the pressing need for change.

There is a model that can prove useful in figuring out what we want, called Optimal Foraging Theory. Biologists have started to look at why different species pick certain sources of food, and disregard others—in some cases even eating things we know to be poisonous or indigestible to them, like when deer eat cat food.

What these scientists have discovered is that most animals engage in a process called *sampling,* in which they eat a little bit of a lot of different things to determine what's the best and most effective food source for them.

Sampling can be an incredibly helpful tool to us, too, as we try to figure out what it is that we want. By trying a bunch of different things, even ones we wouldn't expect to enjoy, we can find out what resonates and narrow the playing field. Zero in on what feels meaningful.

Optimal Foraging Theory includes a number of other behavioral tendencies that can be applied to humans as well, like risk and reward. How much time does a bird spend on a patch of grass seed before flying off to a different patch? It depends on how rich the other patch is likely to be, whether there are more or fewer predators or competitors, how much energy has to be used to travel to the other patch, a whole number of variables that as far as we know, the bird isn't thinking consciously about.

How many similar variables of risk and reward go into our decision making processes, and to what degree are we aware of them? When trying to decide anything from where to pick up dinner to whether to take that new job, there are subtle and subconscious influences within us that inform our choices. If we are able to consciously and mindfully incorporate them into our process rather than sit on the shadowy sidelines, we have a much better chance of success.

So if you don't know where you're headed, take heart. You can begin an adventure without knowing the destination, just by making choices (turn left, turn right) and deciding whether that choice works for you, or whether you'd like to go back and sample a different one. Eventually you will find the one that's right for you, and the excitement will propel you through stage 2.

Identifying the Soul of the Goal

Ultimately Optimal Foraging Theory helps us identify "the soul of the goal". This is the seed that sprouts and grows into the realization of your deepest desire, the concentrated essence of what you want to experience in your daily life.

The more senses you can use when you think about your goal, the more real it will seem to you, and the easier it will be to achieve it. What does it look like? What do you hear? What would it feel like in your body to have achieved it? There might even be scents or tastes involved. Using your physical senses, even in your imagination, helps attune you to your goal.

By the same token it's important to be as specific as possible. Specificity really helps attune your inner compass because it makes that all-important first step clearer. If your goal is general, like "I want to help people" or "I want a better job", the possible first steps are almost infinite. It's totally overwhelming to think about.

If on the other hand your goal is "I want to help people who are struggling with infertility" or "I want a job that will pay me X dollars more per year," your field of view is narrowed, which allows for more clarity.

What are the stories you've been telling about who you are and how you show up in the world? What are the stories you'd *like* to tell? What would you like to be your truth? The stories we tell, and how we'd like to change them, offer a lot of insight into the soul of our goal.

A friend of mine loves to cook. Actually most of my friends love to cook, but this woman in particular revels in it. She thrills to see someone's face light up and then sink into bliss after a taste of her creations. She thought it might be a great idea to make money off this passion and open a restaurant, and discovered that the idea of sharing her food with strangers made her feel exhilarated.

She started the process of getting a business license, looking for space, getting all of the necessary permits and clearances, and she found herself deflating. Losing energy day by day at the prospect of doing everything that was necessary to open a restaurant. Soon all of that exhilaration she'd been feeling was gone. It wasn't owning a restaurant that enthused her, the soul of her goal was sharing food. She started throwing weekly dinner parties, and encouraged her friends to invite their friends, and her goal of "strangers" eating her lovingly crafted meals was realized.

Meanwhile another acquaintance found a different way to fulfill her love of entertaining: For her, it was bringing artists and musicians and academics together for old-fashioned salons, the type that were fashionable in the 18th and 19th centuries in Europe. A couple of times a month she would open her (sizeable) home, have live music, serve coffee and tea and desserts, and visitors would talk and debate with impassioned discourse... it was a lively affair.

Over the course of several years she was asked to hold these more regularly.

She started taking donations to cover the cost. Eventually it grew organically into a sort of private coffeehouse, and she couldn't see any reason to keep it private, so she got her home re-zoned into a commercial space (this was several years ago when such things were easier). It remains to this day a community hub where people can come together to enjoy each other's company and be inspired to titillating conversation.

In both cases, they were surprised by what they ended up with because it's not what they started out looking for. As Joseph Campbell said, "We must be willing to let go of the life we planned so as to have the life that is waiting for us." As long as we remain focused on the soul of the goal, that dot in the center that is the concentrated essence of our desires, then the ideal form can coalesce around it.

If that form seems to be the "wrong" one, as in the case of my friend who found out she didn't actually want to run a restaurant, then we can return to that point of concentration, the focus of our real excitement and enthusiasm, and look for other ways to fulfill it.

Developing the Inner Compass

How do you find those other ways? How do you know which of the experiences you've been sampling is the "right" one, the one you want to put your time and energy and transformational process into?

With practice, we can all attune ourselves to an "inner compass" that points us in the right direction. Essentially driven by clues from our psyches, our compass can guide us on our journeys.

Psychologists and other counselors often use the term *somatics* when talking about these kinds of cues. They've found that our subconscious minds communicate a great deal through our physical bodies. This is where sayings like "I was weak in the knees" or "I felt like my heart was breaking" come from; they're physical symptoms of an emotional or psychological experience.

We're often inclined to overlook such symptoms, particularly if they get in the way of what we have planned, or feel like we "should" do. If we get a little stomachache before sitting down to do a task we really don't enjoy, or our pulse races with fear when confronted with something we're unprepared to deal with, it's common to put mind over matter and continue forward anyway.

But if we start paying more attention to these clues, mindfully aware of the signals our bodies are sending us, then we can use them to our advantage. Sort of like a divining rod, our inner compass helps us feel the path forward with little tremors of excitement when we're pointed in the optimal direction, and a sinking feeling like the wind's gone out of our sails when we're not. Or worse, a deep ache and bone tired response to tasks that we either don't want to engage in or don't have the physical or emotional resources to undertake at the moment.

Certainly we all have obligations. There will always be some things we'd rather not do, but we go ahead and do them anyway for our health and well-being and those of our our families and communities. Ideally we limit such tasks, or find ways to make them more fun or personally meaningful, so that our inner compass isn't thrown off by the act of continually doing things that don't bring us joy. So that we don't forget, and stop listening to it.

Sometimes there is so much noise around us, so many other people's thoughts and feelings and needs and desires that it can be difficult to attune ourselves to that inner knowing. At these times some kind of a meditative practice can be invaluable. A time to slow down, to breathe deeply, to allow all of that noise, all of those "shoulds" to fall away. To be present only to this moment, and what is real and true in the quiet space of wisdom.

If, in that quiet space, you begin to imagine different alternatives, options that you're considering, ideas you've been having, then you can feel how your body responds. Are there pockets of tension? Or lightheartedness? Is there something that you can hardly wait to burst out of the quiet place to go and do? These are your indicators. Trust that the truth, your truth, is within you. That if you listen and honor that voice, you can't help but be happy every day of your life.

Building Your Support System

An important component of the chrysalis you build for yourself in stage 2 is your support system. People you can rely upon to be honest and loving, without judging you or anything that comes up for you in this process.

Some people, when setting about making substantive changes in their lives, find themselves confronted by what Carl Jung called the *Shadow*—a deep, often concealed part of themselves that feeds on fear and doubt and can show us latent beliefs about ourselves and the world that we didn't know we had.

When the Shadow surfaces, having someone around to remind us of our strength and abilities, to provide nourishing feedback and support, is invaluable. A therapist, counselor, or coach, a clergy-member or spiritual leader, someone with some training and experience in helping people navigate their inner darkness is ideal. Friends and family members, people who know us, love us, and want the best for us, can often provide a rousing cheerleading section when we need it the most.

Part of being a member of your support team as you journey through the changes ahead will likely mean they need to accept that their lives may be changed as well. If you're following your inner compass and mindfully putting on your own oxygen mask first, you may not be able to show up for the people around you in the ways you've done in the past. Which hopefully they will embrace, if your happiness is a priority for them. But it's definitely a good idea to have an open conversation about what that might look like, rather than making any assumptions.

You might also want to plan regular check-ins, to ensure you're still on the same page. Whether these are explicitly on the calendar or you hold space to allow them to come up organically, it's worth planning ahead for. People's needs change over time, particularly when they're undergoing a significant transition. Honest, heartfelt communication and negotiation are the key to getting through it effectively and gracefully.

While you're looking around at the members of your community, you might also think about whether any of them have any experience with the kind of changes you're seeking to make in your life. If any of them have already successfully accomplished a goal like yours. If so, perhaps they could offer some guidance as far as how they managed it—perhaps even warn of any pitfalls that may lie in wait on the journey.

You'll never know if you don't ask, and though it can feel a little bit scary to be vulnerable and ask for help, if it gets you where you want to go isn't it worth it? What's the worst that could happen? Is it worse than not realizing your dream at all?

Butterfly Soup

The Pyramids Were Built One Stone at a Time

By this point hopefully you've identified the soul of your goal, you've begun attuning your inner compass, and you've begun pulling in your support system to help you along your journey. You probably don't know what the entire journey will look like; even if you think you do, chances are you'll be surprised along the way.

The most important thing to remember now is that baby steps are still positive steps. All you have to do, all you *can* do, is one thing at a time. Keep moving forward, but be aware that it's really easy to go into overwhelm by making many big changes all at once. It will prove more sustainable to make smaller steps, and be consistent.

Right now, all you need to know is the first step. The first thing you can do to move a little closer to your goal. When you've completed that, then you can look for the next step to take. Bite-size pieces. Baby steps. Deep breaths.

If you're having a hard time figuring out what that first step is, you might try "remembering backwards". Essentially you imagine that you've completed the goal in its entirety, and then think back over all of the steps you might have taken to get there, all the way back to where you are now.

You might also try sitting in your quiet place of wisdom, however that looks to you, and feel the completion of your goal. Again, with as many senses that you can. In doing this you may find that the first step reveals itself to you through your intuition.

As you begin to make your plan, determining each step as the previous is accomplished, and periodically looking farther out for the steps you may need time to prepare for, it's important to build in times for rest and relaxation as well. In yoga it's often said that the corpse pose, in which the body lies still, is the most important one. Our bodies and our psyches need time to integrate the work that has been done, to internalize the changes beneath the surface.

Some of us also need time for rampant rebellion. Periods in which we gleefully turn our backs on our work, to be "bad". Personally, some of my most productive periods have sprung forth after such a time, when I've allowed myself a lengthy video game session or drowned myself in a book. If we mindfully build these times into our practice, then we're less likely to get caught up in self-judgment and recrimination which are both counterproductive and physically toxic. This process is about being happy, not being a workhorse.

In The End, All You've Got Is You

As important as a support system is, at the end of the day, they can't do the work for you. You've got to do the heavy lifting of continuing to move forward through the process in spite of any resistance that comes up (from within you as well as what the world may throw at you) and in spite of the relative comfort "the devil you know" may offer.

This journey takes commitment, renewed on a regular basis. In order to get to the end of it, you have to *know* that achieving your heart's desire is worth whatever conflicts may arise. Feel the commitment ring through your whole body, and infuse your cells with its transformational energy.

As you think about that commitment, do you feel any hesitancy? Do you feel like you're not ready, like maybe the task is too big, too overwhelming? If so, that's totally okay. It doesn't mean you're not actually ready, it just means there are some areas of resistance that are already coming up, and that's completely understandable. You might want to take a quick look at the later sections on Troubleshooting and Resistance, which may help you get a sense of what is holding you back.

You have everything you need to undertake this process, already within you. You have sufficient fortitude. Trust it. Trust yourself and your inner power. Take some deep breaths and allow your conviction to rise to the surface, knowing that you deserve to be happy. You get to experience the full realization of your dreams. You're worth it.

CASE STUDY: Jane, stage 2

Jane had spent so many years thinking of everyone except herself that she didn't know who she was anymore. She had no idea what "happy" looked like, uch less how to find it for herself.

She tried taking an art class, thinking some creative expression might help, but it wasn't nearly as much fun as she'd thought it would be. She thought about skydiving, boxing, scuba diving... but couldn't get interested enough about any of them to even look up online how she might get started.

It got to the point where she would ask people what they were into, what were their hobbies, just so she could find some fresh ideas. Something she could do that was just for her. That let her feel like she was really living, not just supporting the lives of the people around her.

"But the truth is," she said to her husband one night, "this is the one thing I look forward to. My glass of wine at the end of my day."

"Then why don't you do that? Jerry next door makes his own beer, so why don't you make your own wine?"

A flush of excitement rolled up from her toes, and she knew that was exactly what she would do. And she bet Jerry could help her figure out how to get started.

CASE STUDY: Shea, stage 2

In some respects She was ahead of the game, in that they knew they wanted to take action to make the world a better place. But with such a general goal, She had a difficult time figuring out what action to take.

Remembering the old saying, "Be the change you want to see in the world," Shea started with a regular meditation practice every day, in the hopes of "being peace and positive growth". The regimen did seem to help mitigate the constant feeling of dread and overwhelm, and helped Shea make other positive choices throughout the day, but meditating in isolation didn't seem like it would have any kind of global impact.

Shea looked at a bunch of opportunities for activism in their community, but they all seemed to be addressing such a tiny piece of the problem. Shea felt like if they poured their heart and soul into something that wasn't likely to make a big change, ultimately they would be even more disillusioned and disappointed than they were now.

In meditation one night an image popped into Shea's mind of building a house out in the woods with a group of people. Maybe like a

group of volunteers, or an intentional community, Shea wasn't sure but it did have a lot of appeal. If there were a group out there, starting
fresh, not trying to save a decaying society but
instead planting a new seed in that compost,
maybe that was a kind of activism they could get
behind.

It was a huge undertaking, not just finding
such a group and figuring out how to join them,
but also detaching and disengaging from this
other life that clearly wasn't functional. Shea
reached out to all their friends to brainstorm ideas, and to set up cuddle dates for when they
would undoubtedly need them through the process.

Because, as overwhelming as the prospect
was, the idea of being *free* was too delicious to
pass up!

How to recognize it:
➢ You have identified the "soul of your goal", your intention in moving forward.
➢ You feel charged up, and excited to undergo the change in life experience.

Action steps:
✓ Learn as much as you can, about everything related to your goal
✓ Ask for support from your community, let them know your intentions
✓ Make a plan—or at least identify the first step you can take
✓ "Experience" having completed your transformation as often as possible, through visualization, meditation, prayer, artistic pursuits, whatever works for you.

Stage 3: Metamorphosis Begins

For a caterpillar, this stage looks like a nearly complete loss of physical structure into "soup". For us, it might not yet be visibly apparent at all, even though the beginning of an irrevocable change is occurring within us.

Patience, kindness, and gentleness... damn it.

When we finally start taking action in the direction of our dreams, it can be a delicious feeling. All that excitement and exhilaration from Stage 2 propelling us forward, it often feels like nothing stands in our way. Surely the realization of our goal is right around the corner!

Sometimes it really is that easy. But sometimes, the transformative process takes its own sweet time. Certainly we can continue moving forward, but we can't always control the pace. Just like a caterpillar can't take shortcuts on its journey, we can find ourselves at the mercy of forces beyond our control.

There's often an ebb and flow, periods in which a bunch of pieces click into place and we move forward at breakneck speed, and then periods of reflection and planning. Or sometimes other aspects of life pull focus for a while.

When we find ourselves slowed or stymied, it's essential that we not subject ourselves to judgment or recrimination. If we berate ourselves for not moving as quickly or effectively as we'd like (or think we should) it actually impairs the process and slows us down even further.

For those of us who have struggled with depression, it's also common to interpret these downtimes as depressive resurgences. Especially if those negative voices start creeping in. It's easy to feel powerless and hopeless when we can't do what we think we ought to be doing. But when we make a conscious choice to rest, we recover that power. And we can recognize that if we made a choice to stop, we can also choose to start again.

It's important to pay attention to the stories we tell ourselves about our experiences, particularly in situations like these. How easily "I'm so lazy" or "I can never complete anything" becomes our truth. How different to say "I'm taking a break before I get back to work" or "I'm really enjoying this change of pace."

It helps to focus on being gentle and kind to yourself. Practice nourishing self care. Allow yourself to rest and renew to be ready for the next phase of action. You're still "in the soup" regardless of whether it looks like that from the outside. Trust it. Trust yourself.

Butterfly Soup

There is an element of surrender that is difficult for many of us to accept. Allowing the mystery to unfold around and within us. For those of us who only feel safe when we are firmly in control and know exactly what to expect, the unknown can be downright terrifying. But acquiescence can be freeing, too.

I often think of it like white water rafting. Even as we lean into the oars and steer to avoid visible dangers, the current is going to carry us forward at its own pace. It's all about striking that delicate balance between steering and letting go.

But how do you know when to steer? It comes back to your inner compass. Listen to your body. You will begin to notice when it's time to move forward, and when to rest. When to push through resistance, and when to allow that resistance to dissolve of its own accord. Which opportunities to take, and which to pass on. It may take some practice, but the more you listen, the more you'll hear.

Another great use for your inner compass during this stage is to re-assess your plan. Do the steps you've laid out still feel achievable? Or are there some aspects that feel overwhelming? Being honest with yourself is more likely to keep you on track than trying to stick to something that no longer seems reasonable. Check in with yourself periodically to see if there's anything you've been avoiding doing, or if you're experiencing ongoing or extended delays. If so, you might be entering stage 4, or might need to have a look at the Troubleshooting section.

Inhabit Your Vulnerability

In the Introduction I briefly mentioned the "looking good story" many of us tell to ourselves and others, in which we augment, embellish, or hide truths about ourselves in order to have greater appeal.

This tendency is at its core a defense mechanism, one handed down from generations past, from times when the approval of one's community was literally necessary for survival.

But now we live in a different time, and this defense mechanism is not only outdated, it inhibits our health and well-being by encouraging us to live someone else's truth rather than our own. To put others' needs and desires on a higher priority than our own.

As incongruous as it sounds, we are stronger when we are vulnerable. When we lay ourselves open, and are fully in our authentic selves, we are no longer wasting our power or energy on a "pretty" mask. We are more connected to, more aware of our inner compass that orients us on our path. And we no longer have to fear being "caught out" or exposed, because there's no longer anything to catch.

This is not to say that you should tell your whole life story to every stranger you meet. Rather it's an opportunity to re-examine the stories you tell to yourself and your community. Are you regularly standing in integrity, owning your mistakes and reveling in your successes? Do you ever shift attention away from yourself when someone gets too close to discovering something about you that makes you feel uncomfortable? Are you less inclined to call someone else out for behaving inappropriately, for fear of being called "bossy" or otherwise maligned?

The truth is, living in a way that's inauthentic to you is exhausting. It's not sustainable and it definitely detracts from the energy and will and drive you need to see your transformative process through to completion. Plus, it's not fun to live behind a mask that prevents people from seeing the real you. Admittedly taking off the mask increases the chance of some people not liking what they see, but that is nothing compared to the charge you get from the people who do. Who see you for exactly who and what you are, and can't help but love you.

You will also discover how resilient you really are, and how well you can face life's challenges head on, when you're no longer dodging and weaving to protect your cultivated persona. You can ground yourself, breathe, and be honest. You can ask for help when you need it. And as you prove to yourself how strong you really are, you can let some of your fears go, knowing you can handle whatever comes.

Own your integrity. Feel your feelings. Even the "messy" ones. Stand in the raw power of your truth and allow your community to continue showing up for you even when you don't "look good".

You'll be amazed at how the truth really does set you free.

Keep Moving Forward

Much of stage 3 is internal, a process of developing and honing your inner compass and allowing transformation to take hold. But don't lose sight of your ultimate goal; like Odysseus and his crew munching on lotus, it's possible to get waylaid on your journey without realizing it and get stuck for weeks or even months.

Continue looking for opportunities to move toward your goal, even as you're doing your inner work. It may feel a bit like patting your head and rubbing your tummy, or like you're going crosseyed with one eye pointed outwards and the other in, but that's part of why the ebb and flow happens. Figuring out how to be kind and gentle but also stay on task is not easy, but it also doesn't have to happen overnight.

Butterfly Soup

Check in with your body regularly—daily if possible. Are there new areas of excitement that want to be considered? Pockets of distress or resentment that you hadn't been aware of? Maybe what you used to look forward to has now become a boring chore? Don't overlook the clues your body is sending you just because it interferes with your plan. Your plan needs to be able to evolve, as you learn more about yourself.

Remember that Joseph Campbell quote, "You must give up the life you planned in order to have the life that is waiting for you." Forward may turn out to be a different direction than you expected. But if it feels good to your authentic self, that's all that matters.

CASE STUDY: Jane, stage 3

Jane felt so much better once she realized she could make her own wine. Such a small thing, relatively speaking; it wasn't like the laundry was less insurmountable, or her work priorities were any less complicated. But now there was this bright spot in her life that she could look forward to. Something special, that would still be creative and allow her to really put herself into it.

She talked to her neighbor Jerry who home-brewed, and he gave her a list of websites and other resources to get her started. She realized from their conversation that it was a big under-taking; wine is more complicated than beer in a lot of ways, and harder to do on a smaller scale.

But Jane's resolve was not shaken, she was determined to see this through. She spent a lot of time reading, both online and in the library. She joined a number of online communities of home winemakers. Eventually she felt confident enough to plan out the first batch of wine she would make, and researched the best place to buy the various ingredients and pieces of equip-ment.

In fact her determination spread to other aspects of her life as well—she even scrubbed that irritating spot on the living room rug, and scheduled a date night with her husband while their kids were at a sleepover. She just knew everything was going to be okay!

CASE STUDY: Shea, stage 3

Just a few days after deciding to tap out of modern society Shea started to feel better. So many of the conflicts and problems that would ordinarily have stressed them out they now recognized were not their problem.

There was a little guilt around that, an awareness of the privilege and entitlement that allowed them to detach, but Shea hoped that once a new, sustainable community was set up and stabilized then others could be set up all over the world using the same paradigm and reaching out to marginalized folks.

It turned out that a whole lot of intentional communities existed, and some of them were open to new members. A lot of them seemed to be struggling with local lawmakers around issues like zoning, septic, and solar, but Shea figured that was just another sign of the decay and would be fleeting in all likelihood.

Shea found one — an actual "commune" that welcomed people of all genders and orientations, and went for a visit. It was fantastic, such a dream come true! Everyone contributing, operating on a zero waste paradigm, surely this was the answer Shea had been searching for!

How to recognize it:

➢ The excitement builds, and some of the precipitate distress falls away
➢ You feel like you're making progress
➢ Though you're not yet who you're becoming, you're certainly not who you were.

Action Steps:

✓ Be gentle and patient with yourself, while continuing to actively pursue your goal; you can't rush the pro-

cess, but you can maintain momentum

✓ Regularly reassess your plan, to
make sure it still serves your goal

✓ Keep your compass aligned; take the
actions that make you feel excited

Stage 4: Confronting Resistance

Just as the caterpillar's immune system attacks the imaginal cells to activate them, resistance we encounter in our transformational process helps us identify areas for growth and healing, which ultimately hastens the path to our goal if managed appropriatcly. By understanding how these areas of resistance function, we can begin to undermine their influence in our lives.

Form Resists Change

I find it both comforting and frustrating that the primary fundamental reason why it's difficult to transform ourselves is that form resists change. Simple physics. Newton's law of inertia ensures that a significant amount of energy is required to move or alter anything on the physical plane. Frustrating, because there's no getting around it, comforting because it's universal rather than personal.

But the concept doesn't just apply to physical objects. For a variety of reasons ranging from the comfort of the familiar to the myelination of neural axons (the scientific term for how our brains get better at tasks we have practiced) old habits die hard and new ones are often harder to develop.

The good news is once we recognize this basic aspect of resistance we can begin to consciously override it. We can put together a system of actions and rewards that encourage us to break through and build up momentum— because the other side of the inertial coin is that an object in motion tends to stay in motion. So once the groundwork for new habits has been laid (and those axons have been myelinated) it will actually be easier to continue on your trajectory than to go back to the old way of being.

The "You" You Don't See

Another often overlooked source of resistance lies deep within ourselves, what Carl Jung referred to as "the Shadow" or the dark side of our personalities. Other psychologists have differed over the years as to what degree we may or may not be aware of these influences, but most of us have fallen prey at one time or another in our lives.

This is said to be where our "negative" impulses come from: Violence, envy, lust. It's also where our tendencies to undermine ourselves originate, because it's fueled by our fears—both what we're afraid will happen, and what we're afraid *won't* happen.

Theosophist Alice Bailey used instead the term "Dweller on the Threshold," referring to an aspect of the Self that inhibits our progress. We must find a way to work through, work with, or work around our Dwellers in order to accomplish our goals. A friend and I often have "dweller wrangling" conversations, in which we help each other identify the latent beliefs and fears we've been struggling with, to diminish their power.

Whatever we call it, somehow how we have to address the influence of our subconscious minds on our decision making processes. A lot of people, myself included, have had great success with two forms of therapy: Cognitive Behavioral Therapy (CBT) and Eye Movement Desensitization and Reprocessing (EMDR). These help to rewire (re-myelinate) one's neural pathways to diminish negative influences from the subconscious.

It's been suggested that meditation and visualization accomplish a similar goal. Because (as far as we know) the subconscious doesn't process words or language, opening a channel of communication that is visual in nature is thought to be helpful. Studies have shown that higher levels of detail increase the efficiency, particularly when other senses besides sight are involved. So ideally your "visualizations" will include sound, smell, touch, and even taste to be truly effective.

There is a reason "you are your own worst enemy" is such a pervasive saying. Hopefully we can transform that into being "your own best partner" once we get our subconscious minds on board and working with us instead of against us.

Borrowing Trouble

There are so many things to worry about, where does one even begin? Well, if it's not an immediate concern or doesn't have a clear safeguard to be implemented, hopefully one doesn't begin at all.

Butterfly Soup

A lot of us assume there is power in thinking about the future, in preparing ourselves for whatever may arise. But although there is merit in preparation, often we end up caught in a quagmire of needless worry. We work ourselves up into a frenzy about things that may never happen, and end up not moving forward at all as a result.

Frank Herbert, in his series of *Dune* novels wrote a "litany against fear":

I must not fear.
Fear is the mind killer.
Fear is the little death that brings total obliteration.
I will face my fear.
I will permit it to pass over me and through me.
And when it has gone past I will turn the inner eye to see its path.
Where the fear has gone there will be nothing.
Only I will remain.

Over the years I've found this litany incredibly useful, and I'm sure I'm not alone. It's a reminder that my fear inhibits me from thinking effectively. It helps me to allow my fear to move through me, rather than hold me captive. And it assures me that fear is temporary, and *will* pass one way or another. It is not a permanent state of being, even though it may seem so in the moment.

Another method of confronting your fears is to think about the worst thing that could possibly happen—really use your imagination and stretch to almost comical levels. Then ask yourself whether that potential is worse than the certainty of *never* achieving your goals. Of living out your entire life without ever realizing your dreams.

For some people, playing it safe is worth it, they're happy to content themselves with less. But for the rest of us, we might as well roll over and die right now because a life without a dream isn't any life at all. It would be like letting our soul die.

You can also address the relative probabilities of these potential outcomes, and determine if there are any actions you can take ahead of time to prevent them. Usually taking action alleviates the intensity of the fear. Certainly recognizing the near impossibility of a fear coming to pass can limit its effect.

The point is that it's really common to run into some fear-based stumbling blocks. We are hard wired from millennia ago to be afraid of the unknown. It's okay to feel that fear. But it doesn't have to deter you from accomplishing your goals.

Emotional Excavation

Over the years many of us have had opportunities to repress our emotions. We didn't have time for them, or it didn't feel safe in the moment to express them, so we squashed them down and got on with the task at hand.

Unfortunately it turns out that those feelings don't actually go anywhere. They kind of just hang out in our bodies, piling up over time like a big trash heap.

So when we start doing inner work, processing and healing and getting goal-oriented, sometimes those old emotions bubble up and blindside us. We can be suddenly and inexplicably overtaken by rage, or grief, or terror. Even without any apparent trigger, these feelings are just as "real" as those spurred up in the moment.

I call this emotional excavation, because this process is like an archaeological dig where the farther you go the older experiences you uncover. And every one of those old chunks that surface is precious; not only because of what they can teach, but because once they're out they're gone forever, and no longer weigh you down.

It can be daunting to confront, it can feel like a tidal wave threatening to overwhelm a little fishing dinghy. But the effort to keep it all constrained and tucked away pulls from where you need and want to put that energy. It impinges on your integrity and authenticity, so interferes with your inner compass. But most importantly, it prevents you from being the happiest, healthiest you that you can possibly be, and that's a tragedy.

This is one of those areas where a support system is so useful, where being able to reach out to someone who is trained in guiding people through the healing process makes such a difference. You don't have to go through this alone, but you'll be happier when you do finally go through it.

Guilt & Judgment

Of all the ways in which we hold ourselves back and undermine ourselves, guilt and judgment are the most insidious. In large part because they're often automatic responses, and can sneak in so subtly that many of us aren't even aware of it.

But every time you "should on yourself" about what you "should" be doing and aren't, every time you tell yourself you're wrong or bad or not enough, every time you criticize yourself or someone else, you're actually defining for your subconscious what normal looks like, what life should be.

Going back to the myelination of neural axons, when we practice something over and over, our brains create neural pathways to optimize the set of neurons (brain cells) that are involved in order to make that pathway more efficient.

Sort of like a hiking trail: The first time the trail is cut, it takes a lot of time and energy to lay down the path. But when a bunch of people walk down the trail regularly, the path gets worn down and smooth, and much easier to traverse.

If some time passes and nobody walks on it, that trail starts to collect debris. Maybe some tree branches fall onto it, or some rocks roll down from a hill above. So the next time someone takes that path it will be a little harder because it hasn't been used in a while.

Our brains are the same way. If you do something a lot, it becomes easier to do. If you take a break it gets harder to start up again, but eventually it gets easier—particularly if the path had been well used before the break.

So when you spend a lot of time criticizing, your brain gets really good at it. Sometimes there are even "rewards" for doing something so familiar, little surges of neurotransmitters that provide pleasure to reinforce consistency.

But criticism is anathema to the creative process. When we focus on what's bad and wrong, there's no room for what is good and right. Especially not for what is happy. Since that's the ultimate goal, to be happy, those tendencies towards guilt and judgment really need to be phased out.

This is not easy for most people. In our society we are conditioned to emphasize our weaknesses rather than our strengths. This is particularly true for women, who are taught not to put themselves forward, not to think highly of themselves, and to consistently take a subordinate role to men. A lot of that is endemic to the patriarchal nature of our society, but is reinforced through advertising. They have to make us feel like we're not enough in and of ourselves so we have to buy their product.

Butterfly Soup

Start listening to the things you say to yourself. About you and about those around you. Keep a notebook handy and write them down so you can be really clear about your mental habits.

Then start laying down new pathways. When criticisms come up stop yourself and instead say something positive. Something that builds up rather than tears down. Before long if you are consistent, positivity will be your new normal, and you will feel lighter, happier, and more able to tackle life's challenges.

Self Harm Versus Harm Reduction

In these tumultuous and often panic-stricken times, most of us have had to develop coping mechanisms just to get through the day. Sugar, alcohol, shopping, sex, we find some way to bring pleasure into our lives to offset the pain.

Then there are true masochists, people for whom pain really is pleasure.

Either because there is comfort in the familiar, because it's what they feel they "deserve", or because it makes them feel strong to see how much they can withstand.

In many cases these coping mechanisms can be considered "harm reduction". Because stress hormones are so toxic and destructive, anything that diminishes their impact is an improvement. This is one of the reasons a glass or two of wine is said to be so healthy; even though the alcohol is toxic, wine's ability to promote relaxation is so beneficial that the end result is an improvement.

But when a glass or two becomes four or six glasses of wine, the costs begin to outweigh the benefits. The increase of calories, the additional toxins, the dehydration all add up to move the experience from harm reduction to self harm.

Much like a quick shopping trip for some retail therapy can feel good in the moment, it can easily cross over into self harm when that credit card bill arrives!

Then in addition to the physical consequences (the hangover, or that bill) there are emotional consequences as well. All those guilt and recrimination voices, "How could I do that? I'm such a bad person, I have no self control," and we have an extra layer of resistance to fight through before we can get back on track.

As we talked about in stage 3, self care is absolutely necessary. It is essential that you find ways to soothe and satisfy your physical and emotional needs. Sometimes, particularly after undergoing intense emotional work, numbing yourself and tuning out is a completely reasonable response.

But in this as in all things, being mindful and making conscious choices rather than automatically playing out old habits will keep you feeling empowered.

For example, Ernest Hemingway is quoted as having said, "Write drunk, edit sober." Many artists indulge in mind-altering substances when they're being creative. But does it facilitate focus, or distract from the task at hand?

Some people experience harm reduction by being consistent in a routine or by staying safe in a tight-knit community. They find comfort in the familiar. But when does being comfortable serve you and when does it inhibit your progress? If the security of a safety net encourages you to take risks as you seek your heart's desire, that's wonderful. If instead it's allowing you to distract yourself from your true goal, it might be worth re-thinking.

Regardless, it's your body. Your psyche. Nobody knows your truth but you, knows what you need to feel safe and happy as you move through this world. Just be honest with yourself. Stand in your integrity and own your self care in the kindest, gentlest way you can.

Ego Earthquakes

Periodically in life something happens that shakes us to our very core. That changes us inexorably so that we can never be the same again. Losing a parent, or a partner. Being violently attacked. Surviving a horrible accident. Unfortunately these days trauma in one's life is becoming less of an exception, and more the standard. And we all have to find ways to heal.

So many people are struggling with PTSD (Post Traumatic Stress Disorder) with or without a diagnosis. One of the hardest aspects is not being able to trust your sense of danger; not knowing whether the fear and activation response is over something actually dangerous, or whether your mind is playing tricks on you.

Talk about feeling hopeless. On some level you know you've changed, but you're not sure what the ramifications are, and there's no clear sense of how to get back to okay much less thriving. A lot of people report feeling broken, or like something has been ripped out of them and has left a gaping hole.

Fortunately we've come a long way from the "shell shock" victims of WWI that represented our earliest mainstream understanding of trauma recovery. Trauma is no longer a life sentence. There have been tremendous advances in treatment and recovery, including virtual reality applications and new branches of psychotherapy.

It's important that we not judge ourselves for our trauma, because it's not our fault. But it's also important that we get the support and assistance we need to heal so we can begin to trust ourselves again. So our trauma no longer defines us, or prevents us from accomplishing our goals.

Like the Goblin King in the movie *Labyrinth* when Sarah realizes the truth, "You have no power over me." So too the trauma will have no power once the body's innate ability to heal has been activated, and your personal truth has been restored.

"Hell Is Other People"

Sometimes the hardest resistance to overcome is not inside, but around us. Some people in our community may not want us to change. They may try to talk us out of it, demean us, or actively undermine the steps we take toward our goal.

The simplest explanation is that misery loves company. If they're unhappy and not doing anything about it, they want you to be unhappy too. And if you go ahead and work hard and transform your life, then—gasp!—they might have to confront their reality rather than sitting comfortably in the status quo.

Often these people don't even realize what they're doing. They sort of disconnect parts of their psyche from reality as a defense mechanism against being consciously aware of how much pain they're in. And try as you might, you can't make someone be aware against their will, so there's not much you can do for them until they're ready to take action in their own life.

There are also people who "gaslight", so called in reference to a movie about a man who seduces and manipulates a woman into thinking she's crazy so he can control her. This is a form of mental and emotional abuse designed to make the victim feel powerless and often resulting in tremendously low self esteem.

Gaslighters are highly skilled at using words to manipulate people, and are often emotionally mercurial, flashing from doting to angry and back again with seemingly little provocation. Invariably they are certain they are right, and the person they are gaslighting is wrong—and they will twist facts if necessary to maintain this belief, until the victim can no longer trust their own senses much less their intuition. Needless to say if there is someone in your life who gaslights you, they will make it harder to accomplish your goals (particularly if it means they lose some of their control over you).

But some people are just struggling with their own resistance, dancing with their own Shadow, and those struggles end up slopping over onto the people around them. Maybe they've become extra needy, wanting extra support and encouragement while they work through their stuff, and they don't realize the impact they're having on others.

One of the most effective tools for addressing resistance that comes to us from other people is our boundaries. It's almost cliché, but truly deciding for yourself what you are and are not willing to give, what you are and are not willing to be exposed to is one of the best ways you can empower yourself on your journey. And then once you decide, stick with it. Own your truth and recognize that you deserve to have your truth honored.

Part of standing in integrity, in authenticity, is holding your own space. Maintaining those boundaries. Like in the movie *Dirty Dancing*, "This is my dance space, that's your dance space. No spaghetti arms!" When we each stand in our power and accountability, we are so much stronger—separately and together. Oftentimes "no" is the most important word in our vocabulary.

It's up to you to set your own priorities, and determine to what degree you'll allow others to impede your progress. Sometimes the tradeoff is totally worth it, but be mindful that sometimes our conditioning (our Shadow) tells us it's worth it when it really isn't.

If you think you might be being subjected to abuse, please reach out to someone (even anonymously if necessary) to get some outside perspective and support. But also remember the immortal words of Eleanor Roosevelt, "No one can make you feel inferior without your consent."

CASE STUDY: Jane, stage 4

When Jane started to become a winemaker, or at least to make her own wine, she'd had no idea how much chemistry would be involved. How much math. And though she hated to admit it, she'd had a terrible time trying to get through those subjects in school.

But she knew she couldn't give up. This was the first thing she'd wanted in years, so she couldn't listen to those little voices in her head that were trying to convince her that she would fail, that she'd never be good enough. Instead she enrolled in some classes at the local community college, so she could get the foundational knowledge she'd need in order to move forward.

Fitting classes into an already full schedule was a challenge. She and her husband talked about it, and he stepped up and took over a lot of the household responsibilities (and finally understood why she had complained about the laundry all these years!) But Jane's friends were really missing her.

When they finally did get together something felt off; Jane wasn't interested in getting drunk and catty anymore, she would much rather be constructive and proactive, helping the other mothers who were struggling rather than tearing them down behind their backs.

Her friends told her she'd changed, and Jane decided she was glad about that. She had wanted a change, and even though she hadn't realized this would be one of the side effects, being happier just felt better. It was worth it. She hoped it didn't mean the end of those friendships, but she was prepared to face whatever came, knowing that she was making healthy choices for herself.

CASE STUDY: Shea, stage 4

After having lived alone for many years, Shea found it difficult to negotiate life with so many other people around. They were glad to be released from so many stresses that had weighed them down, but now every day there were *new* stresses. A raccoon had gotten into the hen house and wreaked all kinds of havoc. Some weird blight had just about wiped out the kale and broccoli in the garden. And this guy Sam just *would not* stop telling everyone what to do, even in areas that were not his expertise.

Meditation continued to be a big part of Shea's daily routine, and consciously practicing gratitude. Yes, a chicken was killed along with a number of eggs, but most of the chickens had survived. The blight hadn't taken out the cauliflower or chard. And everyone was annoyed with Sam.

The members of the commune decided to implement some communication strategies to alleviate the distress they were all feeling. This would include weekly meetings of the entire group to reflect on the efficacy of the strategies, and to modify them if necessary.

Shea began to wonder if they had made the right choice, moving out to the middle of nowhere with no electricity and virtually no contact with the outside world. Sure it felt great to be away from all the toxicity, but was this really activism or was it a cop out? Was anything the group was doing going to mean anything in the long run?

The more they thought about it the more Shea felt plagued with doubt. And yet couldn't see another more appealing option. So they sat with those questions, and went to go muck out the goats again.

How to recognize it:
- ➢ Progress slows or stalls
- ➢ Worry, doubt, and limiting beliefs begin to creep in
- ➢ Your goal begins to feel unattainable

Action Steps:
- ✓ Recognize that the resistance is a totally natural part of the process, and it doesn't have to control you; you are in charge of your actions, and your responses to outside influences.
- ✓ Try to identify where the resistance comes from, and process through the root cause
- ✓ Ask for help. Other people around you may have already found solutions to the issue you feel confronted with.
- ✓ Spend some time with the Troubleshooting section, if there are specific

areas of resistance that you need more guidance around.

Stage 5: Breakthrough

The fully realized butterfly ("imago") breaks free from the now too-small constraints of the chrysalis by stretching its wings. Victory, success, the final completion of our goal isn't always easy or apparent to us, but every breakthrough—every win —is worthy of being celebrated. Whether it's the first success on a long road to your larger goal, or the end result you've been striving for, it's important to take a breath, admire the view, and pat yourself on the back for what you've accomplished.

Engage the Win

Successfully overcoming resistance of any kind is a victory and deserves to be celebrated. Some of us have a tendency to play down or write off "minor" triumphs because they're "not a big deal". But if you allow yourself to really be present to what you've accomplished, really feel it, then you can bolster your self esteem as well as diminishing the power that form of resistance will have on you in the future.

Just think about all the times you have succumbed to that resistance in the past, or all of the other people who may still be struggling with it. Truly, there is no such thing as a small victory. Revel in your success!

Particularly as for most of us the path to our heart's desire is a long one, it's important to be able to find joy in the process, not just the outcome. To enjoy the journey, not just the destination. Celebrating is a fantastic way to renew your vigor and excitement, to keep you motivated to continue.

As you do so, be mindful of what Dr. Brené Brown calls "foreboding joy," a process by which we subvert and subjugate our happy feelings by "dress rehearsing tragedy". She says that because being present to our joy requires us to be vulnerable, we will often offset the experience by focusing on what horrible thing may be lurking right around the corner. She encourages us to practice gratitude in these moments, to help ourselves remain open.

You might consider keeping a victory journal, writing down all you accomplish, the hurdles you successfully leap. It can be a really useful tool, so you can go back and review later. Especially if you find yourself wrestling with self doubt down the line, you can turn to this list and say, "See? I did all this! I'm actually pretty awesome and talented!"

Then too if there are areas of resistance that you've struggled with for a long time and are likely to come up again, you might jot down a couple of notes about what you did to be victorious this time to help future you be victorious as well.

Butterfly Wings Need Time To Dry

Sometimes, even after the biggest victories, the celebration that's called for is a time of quiet reflection. A moment of peace. A time to feel the stillness that happens when the out breath is complete and the in breath hasn't yet begun.

Failure only happens when we give up, when we stop trying. If you're still plugging away that's not failure, just a lesson learned along the way. So if you haven't ended up where you wanted, or you don't want where you've ended up, it just means you're not yet at the end of your journey.

Remember that "two steps forward one step back is a Cha Cha." Rather than allowing yourself to get mired in frustration, think about all you've learned and how much easier it will be to move forward from here with so many more tools at hand.

Try not to let any old programming or negative thinking convince you that you haven't accomplished anything meaningful. The Shadow, the Dweller on the Threshold, these voices can be pernicious and rob us of our hope. But if you set a firm intention to continue through to the accomplishment of your dream, and follow through, you can prove those voices wrong.

Some of us have also found, much to our chagrin, that once we've climbed the peak we set out for we discover another peak rising behind it just begging to be crested. As much as we'd like to sit and rest awhile, our adventurous spirits won't let us pause for long.

It is always okay to change your mind about what victory looks like to you. It is always okay to try out something new and see how it feels—and then go back to your first idea, or move on to something else that you haven't tried yet. You are limited only by your imagination and willingness to think creatively, allowing yourself and your plan to evolve.

And keep checking on your inner compass. Before you know it you'll be back at stage 1, ready for a whole new change!

CASE STUDY: Jane, stage 5

It took much longer than Jane had expected before she was able to uncork her first bottle of wine, but it was totally worth it. Not only had she found a new level of passion for wine, but she and her husband had grown closer through the process, and her self esteem had improved dramatically. She shared that first bottle with him, late one night after the kids were in bed, and they talked about how grateful they were to have gotten to this point in their marriage.

The second bottle Jane decided to share with her friends, who she hadn't seen in a while. She was a little nervous after everything that had happened, but was pretty sure they would accept the peace offering as justification for her decisions. After all they had been friends for years, surely they could figure out how to work through this hiccup.

But then it turned out her words had been an inspiration to the whole group! They now were all working towards their own goals and aspirations (and trying to break the cattiness habit). They all toasted to how far they'd come, how far they had yet to go, and the friendships that would see them through.

The third bottle she thought she might use as a "resumé" at a local winery, see if she could get a job that didn't just meet her needs, but fueled her soul.

CASE STUDY: Shea, stage 5

Over time Shea came to realize that the source of their distress was within. That they could have figured out how to be happy "back in the world" if they had really wanted to, if they had really tried, but at the time it just hadn't seemed possible. And maybe that was okay.

Butterfly Soup

Besides it was easier to be happy out underneath the trees, or frolicking with the newborn animals. And what did "making a difference" really mean? Maybe the point of life is to be happy, and to make others happy to the best of your ability. Certainly a lot of the spiritual doctrines suggested that, and it seemed as good a place to start as any.

Shea started to think about writing a book about their experiences and discoveries. Maybe that was the "difference" they'd been seeking all along.

How to recognize it:

➢ The resistance has fallen away; you feel lighter and more in control

➢ There's a pause for you to catch your breath

Action Steps:

✓ Pat yourself on the back! Overcoming resistance is hard, but you succeeded!

Troubleshooting

Sometimes the system doesn't work the way it's supposed to. Sometimes we can't even get from stage 1 to stage 2, much less to 5. Just like with computers, sometimes inexplicable error messages pop up or the system crashes, and we have to figure out why. The solutions are unique, depending on what other hardware and software we have installed, so some basic troubleshooting steps help us identify the problem and see if we can get back online.

Of course each person's experiences are unique, including the symptoms of some of these ailments. But these are some of the most common I've seen and experienced.

1. Do you feel safe?

Do you perceive dangers around you physically, emotionally, or spiritually? There is an evolutionary imperative that if our brains think we're in danger, they will focus every effort on getting us safe again. They will pump stress hormones to aid us in fight or flight, and these neurochemicals prevent us from being aware of anything else going on in our bodies.

Other high stress aspects can figure in here too, even if you don't think of them as "dangerous." A long, onerous commute. A boss who harangues you on a regular basis. Regularly missing meals without compensating for blood sugar fluctuations. Ongoing difficulties in relationships. Watching the ever-increasing violence and other hardships on the news. So many normative components of daily life in this culture actually prevent your brain from functioning effectively, but we develop a secondary defense system to keep us from noticing it, because we "have" to do these things.

Interestingly, studies have shown people experiencing high levels of stress are less likely to take risks. If the path to your heart's desire involves putting yourself on the line either physically or emotionally, and you are experiencing the physiological effects of stress, you will likely find ways to avoid taking moving forward without even realizing it.

Similarly if you're feeling overwhelmed by daily life, then you might not have the emotional or physical resources to take on anything else regardless of how desperately you might want to. Christine Miserandino introduced Spoon Theory, a way to talk about how difficult life can be for people with chronic pain or illness, particularly those maladies that are invisible to other people. When you start out each day with a limited number of "spoons," and each task or action costs at least one spoon, sometimes you run out of spoons before you even get through life's necessities. In such cases, chasing a dream can feel like a luxury you can't afford.

You deserve to feel safe. You deserve to feel supported. You deserve to be functioning at your highest potential. You deserve to sail through the transformative process and experience your heart's desire.

How to recognize it:

➢ Anxiety—Tight chest, shaking hands, queasy stomach.

➢ Anger—Regularly flaring up, almost uncontrollably.

➢ Depression—Curling up in a ball and wanting the world to go away.

➢ Asthma—In some cases, our bodies somatize fear into our lungs in a way that mimics the symptoms of asthma, but in this case often inhalers are ineffective.

➤ Indigestion—While this is sometimes due to poor nutrition, high stress definitely contributes.

➤ Chronic pain—the neurochemical cortisol can linger in our muscles and organs, causing inflammation and physical distress.

Action Steps:

✓ Get yourself safe. Whatever that looks like to you. It might be leaving a problematic relationship or job, or standing up for yourself. Carpooling instead of commuting solo, or using it to listen to audiobooks and podcasts to broaden and brighten your mind.

✓ Bring in your support system, that's what they're there for. Ask for help. You deserve it.

2. Are you nutritionally deficient?

The definition of nutrition has gotten muddled in our society, due in large part to the influences of agri-business, big pharma, fast food and factory food, and the diet industry. There are so many conflicting messages about the "right" way to be healthy, many of them essentially propaganda to get us to reach for our pocketbooks.

The thing is, if our brains don't have the nutritional resources they need, then they'll often send out confusing or misleading signals that make it difficult to be aware of, much less trust our internal compass. I often recall with amusement one of my intuitive friends saying, "I can't tell if there's a disturbance in the energy fields around me, or if I just need a sandwich." It was funny at the time, but it also illustrates how being hungry can throw off one's ability to effectively recognize physical or emotional cues. And can't we all identify with being "hangry"?

Even if we're eating regularly, we might not be getting the specific nutrients we need to be effective. Jon Gabriel's book *The Gabriel Method* outlines some really useful basics for how to make sure your body gets what it needs, without having to go on a restrictive diet. In it he suggests that we approach changes in our food consumption from an additive perspective, rather than detractive. Since the goal is to find a sustainable approach, it doesn't make sense to cut out your favorite foods that you would miss and want to "cheat" with. Instead, add in some core necessities like multi-colored veggies, omega-3 and omega-6 fatty acids, and good protein. Then if you still want that ice cream or cheeseburger, you can enjoy it without self-destructive guilt. He says a lot more, and suggests other more robust nutritional changes, but adding important nutrients is a fantastic first step.

Some prescription drugs can also affect motivational or developmental processes, particularly those designed to help us cope with mental issues like anxiety and depression. This is not to say that they're not useful, or that people shouldn't take them. But if you are taking a pharmaceutical and are also feeling like you lack the energy or momentum that you would like, it might be worth discussing with your health care professional. Sometimes it feels easier to address the symptom with a pill instead of rooting out the underlying cause, even though it's not as productive in the long run. Your body is your own, and you should use whatever tools work for you, but if they don't work the way you want them to there are alternatives.

Another set of issues to think about discussing with a health care or nutritional professional is inflammation, infection, and auto-immune disorders. A lot of people in these modern times suffer from these issues without even realizing it. We have come to assume that as we get older we'll experience a fair amount of physical distress, and just sort of go along with it, medicating as needed. In many cases, changing the food we eat or how we prepare it can ameliorate these symptoms, resulting in a lifestyle we never thought possible. For example, many people report significant shifts after taking probiotics for a few weeks. It's amazing how far reaching the effects of improved gut health are.

Of course the impact of regular exercise cannot be overlooked. There have been so many studies documenting the positive effects of even a casual stroll once or twice a week. That being said, it is massively counter-productive to judge or shame yourself if you're not as active as you feel like you "should" be. Do the best you can, be gentle with yourself, and hold space for the possibility of change. This process is about increasing the joy in our lives, not about yet another source of guilt.

It's time that we reclaim our notion of health for ourselves, with focus on what makes us truly happy and filled with energy to get through the day and accomplish our goals.

How to recognize it:

➢ You're not getting multiple colors of fruits and vegetables several times a week, omega-3's and omega-6's at least once a day, and lean protein several times a day.

➢ Most of your food is packaged and made with chemicals you can't pronounce.

➢ You're taking prescription (or recreational) drugs that leave you feeling empty or powerless.

➢ You're often in physical pain that is not the result of an injury.

Action Steps:

✓ Focus on adding in food you think of as healthy, rather than subtracting unhealthy ones. The process is more sustainable if you don't feel like you're missing out.
✓ Explore finding a different coping mechanism.
✓ Be mindful of the stimulants and depressants that you consume, and their impact on your nervous system.
✓ Do some research to find out if any of the things you eat and drink might be causing inflammation or allergic reactions.
✓ Look for a physical activity that brings you joy, something you're excited to get out and do.

3. Are you engaging in negative self talk?

Sometimes we say things to and about ourselves that we would never allow someone to say about our best friend. Things like "I'm so stupid," or "I'm such a loser." Unfortunately, saying these kinds of things even if we "don't mean it" not only whittles down our confidence, but can actually affect our nervous system and have a strong negative impact physically.

It's understandable behavior. Many of us subconsciously want to say worse things to ourselves than others might say, because it will hurt less if we're not blindsided by the unexpected. Or maybe we've internalized something that someone in a position of power said to or about us, and it became a "lesson" in who we are or how the world works.

Another kind of negative self talk that we might not even be aware of comes from our limiting beliefs. These are often subtle messages we tell ourselves about how and why we can't have what we want. Also often coming at an early age from people in positions of power in our lives, it can take some diligence to identify these beliefs because they are so intertwined with the fabric of our reality.

As an example, I worked with someone who really wanted to sing in a band, but "knew" she couldn't, because she had been told she was a horrible singer. It never occurred to her that a vocal coach could help her develop that skill, because she didn't know they existed. Instead, she had resigned herself to living life without ever experiencing her dream, because she believed it was forever out of reach due to her innate "lack of talent".

I myself was affected by the limiting belief that I could never write this book, because I'd never done anything like it before. Other people were writers, not me. How would I even go about such a thing? Once I was aware of the belief that was holding me back, I could recognize that a lack of experience didn't need to deter me, because everyone was a first-timer at some point. But first I had to "hear" my objections to the possibility, so I could know how to rewrite that story.

Negative self talk of any kind undermines our ability to accomplish our heart's desire, to be happy. It's in our best interest whenever possible to root out that behavior, and instead give ourselves positive messages of confidence and self love.

How to recognize it:
➤ You say things to or about yourself you would not allow someone to say to a child or a friend.

➤ When problems arise, your immediate reaction is to self-recriminate, rather than to address the problem.
➤ You're harder on yourself than others are, or friends often tell you to "take it easy".
➤ You think that you can't have, or don't deserve, your heart's desire.

Action Steps:

✓ Each time you catch yourself saying something negative, immediately counter with something positive to break the pattern.
✓ Develop affirmations of positive aspects about yourself.
✓ Put up signs around your space with positive messaging about you and your goals.
✓ Set aside some time to let your mind wander while thinking about your desire, and listen for any messaging that suggests it is unattainable.

✓ Seek out professional counseling to explore the origin of the negativity.

4. Are you allowing faith to supersede action?

Marx is often quoted as having called religion "the opiate of the masses," but faith in something larger than ourselves can be useful in many ways. We can be more inclined to set our fears aside and take risks, knowing that someone will break our fall. We have easier access to a built-in community of like-minded folks who can provide support. Our minds can be broadened even as our spirits are lifted, encouraging us to explore different ways of being in the world.

The downside of some religious convictions is that if God or Allah or the Universe will provide, then there is no reason for us to take action on our own behalf. Prayer and meditation and visualization and affirmations are all important and useful tools as we move towards our heart's desire, but are not enough on their own.

Like the modern parable of the person standing on the roof of their house during a flood, praying to be saved. First a rowboat comes to rescue them, then a police motor boat, and finally an evacuation helicopter, but each time the person says, "No thanks, I have faith that God will save me." Ultimately the house collapses and the person dies. Once in heaven they ask, "God, why didn't you save me?" To which God responds, "I sent you three ways to get off of that house, what else were you looking for?" We must take action in our lives and vigilantly watch for opportunities as they present themselves.

In addition, when we engage in our spiritual practices, it's important to note the difference between rote and ritual. It's easy to get into a routine, a practice where we just say the words, or generically visualize what we want to experience, but without putting our whole self into it, we won't get much back out of it.

We need to allow the mystical in. To use all of our senses so our brains are engaged on several levels. To feel the Truth and the joy of our desire, all the way out to our fingertips and down to our toes. (If your goal doesn't inspire that level excitement for you, if you don't feel it that viscerally even after a fair amount of practice, then you might want to spend some time thinking about troubleshooting step #5, Maybe it's Not Your Goal).

This is particularly relevant for people who have been working with the Law of Attraction, acting as if and waiting for their goals to be fulfilled. Like most practices, there is truth at the core of it, but for many of us it can appear to be a free ride. The promise of riches without any hard work, somewhat akin to a pyramid scheme.

Attuning yourself to your inner compass is not the same as following your bliss, in large part because sometimes doing what's right for you isn't blissful. Sometimes it hurts a lot, but for whatever reason, hurting a little bit now will lead to less pain in the future, or even to great joy and freedom. Sometimes putting on your own oxygen mask first means someone else in your life feels let down, and there's nothing blissful about that. Sometimes we have to dig out a conflicting belief deep in our subconscious, that originated in fear or pain. That's often not a pleasant experience, but the feeling of freedom that results is so worth it.

To achieve your heart's desire you have to be truly authentic and honor your personal Truth. It's not as easy as some doctrines may lead us to believe, but it is infinitely more successful.

How to recognize it:

➢ You think your deity or the center of your spiritual power wants you to not take action.

➢ You've been praying or meditating on the same subject for months or even years, but little or nothing has changed in your life.

➢ Your spiritual practice feels flat, or you aren't getting what you need or want out of it.

➢ Your belief structure or spiritual practice has left you feeling abandoned or disillusioned.

Action Steps:

✓ Have a dialogue with your deity, representative, or center of your spiritual power to ask why you shouldn't take action. Ask for what you need (e.g. your rowboat as in the parable above) and re-affirm your willingness to be an active participant in the process..

✓ Keep an eye out for ways in which you can take steps to move forward.

✓ Explore what feels mystical or magical to you, to bring a deeper, more ritualistic quality to your spiritual practice.

✓ If all else fails, explore a different religious or spiritual practice, or even take a break and try none at all for a while to see how that resonates for you.

5. Maybe it's not your goal?

There is an evolutionary imperative for us to please the people around us, particularly those in positions of power. Thousands of years ago, when humanity lived exclusively in tribes, we had to make sure that the tribe accepted us because to be kicked out meant almost certain death. The people who succeeded at pleasing their community lived and passed down their genetics, and to a certain degree their behaviors.

In modern times we can survive without the acceptance of others, but we still have that built-in tendency. Plus, there are so many pressures to conform, to fit in, to "do our part". To follow in the footsteps of a parent, or to live the dream they were never able to achieve. But doing so is often not authentic for us. If it's not authentic, it's not sustainable.

Also, some of us outgrow our goal without realizing it, continuing to move forward after it's no longer meaningful or relevant for us, just out of habit. It can be almost heartbreaking to let an old goal go, particularly one we've held on to for a long time. If that goal has become part of how we define ourselves, then who are we without it? But the heartbreak of separation is temporary, and makes room for greater joy.

Either way, it doesn't serve you to work towards somebody else's heart's desire, even if the somebody else is an outdated version of you. Focus back in on the soul of your goal (discussed in Stage 2, Building the Chrysalis) and make sure your goal is your own.

How to recognize it:

➤ The thought of your desire being achieved doesn't fill you with excitement, exuberance, enjoyment, energy.

➤ You find yourself plodding through the necessary steps and actions, but your heart isn't in it.

➤ You sabotage yourself, making it impossible to move forward.

➤ You consistently procrastinate or put off taking action.

Action Steps:

- ✓ Let this goal go, and go back to stage 2 to find what is authentically yours.
- ✓ Find an aspect of it that does make you feel excited, and focus on that.

6. Are you addicted to the flush of a new project?

New ideas and new projects are generally very exciting. We feel filled with creative energy, anything is possible, we are revitalized...and we haven't yet run up against any resistance or anything "hard." For some of us, coming up with a new idea is much easier than dealing with our resistance, so we jump from project to project without seeing anything through to completion.

There's nothing necessarily wrong with that, if that's what truly makes you happy. But if you feel even an iota of self-recrimination or judgment about "giving up" or "failing," then you owe it to yourself to look at your lack of follow through squarely, and explore how to get back on track. You deserve to get all the way through to experiencing your heart's desire.

The first step of course is to recognize the pattern of behavior, acknowledge that you've tended to stay with an idea only during the honeymoon phase. Then rather than making a conscious choice to stop pursuing it, because it doesn't work for you (which would be *sampling* as seen in stage 2, Building the Chrysalis) you have instead floated away from it unintentionally, as a result of subconscious influence.

On the bright side, once you see what's happening, you get to make choices. It's no longer something that happens to you, or something that's innate or intrinsic to you as a person, it's something you can take charge of. Get the better of.

Butterfly Soup

Pick the project that you're most excited about, and make a plan. A schedule. Dig in to stage 2 and develop your tools and strategies. Build into your life times on a regular basis that you will commit to working towards your goal. Then, if you find yourself not adhering to your schedule, ask yourself why. Are you encountering resistance (stage 4)? Is it not your goal (Troubleshooting #5)?

Sitting with the muse in the early stages of the creative process is always a delight. But the muse will stick around for the end of the project, if you do.

How to recognize it:
➢ You have many projects begun, but not completed.
➢ You feel excitement at the outset, but then get bored or lose interest.
➢ You struggle with self loathing around a perceived lack of follow-through.

Action Steps:

✓ Apply your mindfulness techniques. Pay attention. Make choices.
✓ Allow yourself to discover where your resistance is coming from.
✓ Re-write any story you may have been reinforcing around being a "quitter" or a "failure." You've got this! Tomorrow's a new day.

7. Are you stuck in a catch-22?

Many of us have found ourselves confronting a catch-22 in our lives, a paradox of sorts. Like, you have to have had a job, so you can prove you can do a job, in order to get a job. But how can you get a job if you've never had a job? Around and around you go on a mental circle, never finding the starting point that says, "Here, do this thing..."

That mental circuit often results in limiting beliefs and ultimately despondency, because it seems that your goal will be forever beyond your reach, unattainable. After all, if you can't find the beginning of the path, how can you walk down it?

If you believe a task is impossible, then it becomes impossible, because you've given up before you've really started. It's a totally normative response, that frustration and even fury that makes us throw up our hands in surrender to the inevitable. That makes us believe we are powerless in the face of overwhelming odds, so why even bother?

The good news is, there's usually a way to circumvent a catch-22. You are not powerless if you are willing to think creatively, and stick with it. If someone else has accomplished your goal, you can too; find out what they did, how they managed to succeed, and emulate that in your own life. Ask around. Research on the internet. Collect as much information as you can. Stay in stage 2 (Building the Chrysalis) as long as you need to, to find what you're looking for.

It may not be easy, few things worth having are. It may take harder work, or more networking, or a longer period of growth and development than you're open to. Only you can decide what works for you, how much you're willing and able to give. Maybe at some point the ends no longer justify the means, and you decide to move on to another goal. There's no shame in that.

Just don't give up on your heart's desire as being "impossible" until you know for certain that it actually is.

How to recognize it:

➢ You're unable to find that first step to take on the path to your goal.

➢ You've identified a chicken/egg scenario in which something paradoxical is required for you to move forward.

Action Steps:
- ✓ Do research. Find out how other people have voided the paradox.
- ✓ Brainstorm. Give yourself the space and time to think outside the box and develop a creative solution that's uniquely yours.
- ✓ Play around with "remembering backwards". Imagine your goal, then work backwards step by step in your mind through every stage until you get to where you are now.

8. Are you navigating multiple simultaneous goals?

There is so much to see and do in this life, it's easy to want to do it all at once. Certainly in this post-modern world where everything moves so quickly, it's easy to feel like we have to. But given that this transformational process is all about finding the stillness, the quiet, so we can listen to the messages our bodies and psyches are sending us, trying to do several things at once can really interfere with that process.

Which is not to say you can't have multiple goals, or even that you can't work toward more than one goal at a time. But often, if there are too many pots on the stove, none of them get the attention they need and deserve. Multitasking is the bane of mindfulness, and as a result, often prevents people from moving swiftly along their path.

If you do find yourself with several goals, allow space and time to be present with each of them one at a time. When you're planning your path and making your schedule, slot in different times for each, to make sure you can give your full attention in the moment. As an example, I had a client who was working on a novel and a cookbook at the same time, while working a 9-to-5 job. She decided to work on the novel on Mondays, Tuesdays, and Saturdays, and the cookbook on Wednesdays and Sundays. They were both completed within the year.

Your dreams are important. You should dream big and often. But if you have many dreams, make a plan. Allow yourself to really focus, and you'll get there.

How to recognize it:

➢ Frantically trying to make sure multiple goals continue to move forward.

➢ Feeling like your goals aren't getting the attention they need, because you have too many.

➢ Lower quality or less progress than you'd like, due to splitting your focus.

Action Steps:

✓ Make a plan. Ensure that each of your goals get some time regularly, and focus exclusively on that one goal during that time.

✓ Consider putting off working toward one goal, until another one is completed.

9. Do your fears feel overwhelming?

Going back to Frank Herbert's "litany against fear" from stage 2, "Fear is the mind killer." I think most of us can agree that though our imaginations can run wild when we are afraid, conscious decision making becomes much more difficult. What's more, with all the stress chemicals flooding our system during times of fear, it becomes virtually impossible to get an accurate read on our inner compass, because there are so many different signals happening at once.

It's totally natural to feel afraid of a negative outcome, and it's generally a good idea to prepare for any eventuality. But when we focus more on what are afraid will happen than we focus on what we want to happen, we're diverting energy and making it harder to reach our goal.

Plus, if a fear lingers too long, we have a tendency to believe that it is a fact. We subconsciously want to prove that we were right to fear—or worse, prove someone else right, if it's something they've warned us against for years. A loved one saying, "You'll never amount to anything," for example.

Ideally, rather than thinking of what may go wrong, we spend the majority of our time and mental energy on the positive outcome, on our actual goal, the heart's desire. Fears may pop up, and can provide useful information for our journey. Write them down, along with any ideas about how to address or avoid them, and then intentionally focus your mind back on the successful completion of your goal, to get back on track.

Some fears are pernicious, coming to mind over and over again, and that's OK. Go through the same process each time, jot down anything new, and focus back on "feeling" your heart's desire with as much detail as possible. Eventually those fears will lose some of their power and intensity. In the meantime, you won't have gotten derailed from your trajectory.

How to recognize it:

➢ Fears come into your consciousness that keep you from moving forward.

➢ You spend your time thinking about what you don't want to happen in your life, rather than what you would like to experience.

➢ Your life has become about avoiding negative outcomes, rather than experiencing happiness and excitement.

Action Steps:

✓ Write down your fears and any mitigating action, then try to put them out of your mind and focus on the positive.

✓ Check in with someone you trust to determine if your fears are realistic, or the product of your social conditioning.

✓ Remind yourself of all the times things haven't gone your way, and how you managed them. Odds are, if you've done OK in the past, you'll do even better in the future.

10. Are you disregarding your progress and accomplishments?

Particularly when we've lived for and worked towards a goal for a long time, it's easy to fixate on the fact that we haven't accomplished it yet and overlook the wonderful forward movement we've made. In the immortal words of Carrie Fisher, "Instant gratification takes too long!"

In the absence of completion, we can begin to feel as though we've failed, allowing our energy to plummet and our goal to seem farther away than ever.

A similar obstacle is Imposter Syndrome. The principle was introduced by Dr. Pauline R. Clance and Suzanne A. Imes, to describe people who "are highly motivated to achieve," while they "live in fear of being 'found out' or exposed as frauds." Women seem to struggle more with this, perhaps since our society has historically encouraged us to make less of our accomplishments and take a back seat to our male counterparts.

It's important that we honor our victories, large and small. That we revel in our skills, our strengths, and our areas of personal growth. They show us not only how far we've come, but also help us to keep moving forward. Sometimes progress comes in fits and starts, and sometimes all in a rush. But even the tiniest of baby steps is meaningful, if it's followed by another one, and then another.

If this is an area of struggle for you, if you feel like you're "not the type of person" who gets to achieve their heart's desire regardless of how hard you work towards it, or if you're just about to give up out of frustration that you haven't yet gotten to the end of your journey, take heart. You are not alone. Lean on your support system, people who can tell you how much progress they've seen you make, and cheerlead you on your way. A journal of wins is also useful, so you can go back and look at your accomplishments whenever your confidence slips.

How to recognize it:

➤ You feel like you've failed, because you're not yet where you want to be.
➤ You feel like you don't deserve to be where you are in life, much less where you want to go.
➤ Your patience is wearing thin, and it seems like giving up is preferable to struggling on.

Action Steps:

✓ Reach out to the people you can count on, and ask them to help you see the ways in which you've been making progress.

✓ Put together a list of all the new skills and/or strengths you've developed since you started your journey.

✓ Keep a victory journal, writing down every success—particularly baby steps—and read it as often as you need. When you do, try to feel the truth of those wins, and let them chase away the darkness.

In parting...

The truth is, we're never done changing and growing. These five stages continue to cycle throughout our lives and various goals, propelling us forward to become better, stronger people. And though that can seem daunting, like the work is never done, there is some freedom and relief in understanding the process and how it shows up in our lives.

As you spend more time with it, and pay attention to what you're feeling, you'll recognize the symptoms of the various stages more quickly and move through them more confidently.

In fairness I have to acknowledge that Resistance is no joke. Especially when it stirs up old wounds, traumas, and stories that have lain dormant for years. I cannot stress enough the importance of a support system to help work through that stuff. We are social animals, and don't function well in isolation. Often friends and family are sufficient, but sometimes professional and trained guidance makes all the difference.

Dream big. You are limited only by the stories you tell.

Breathe. Allow yourself to be present to the flow.

Keep moving forward. Every step is meaningful.

You've got this!

About the Author

(in her own words)

I'd always had a burning curiosity to understand the how's and why's of the world, which led to a self-guided education in psychology, anthropology, political science, economics, literature, and metaphysics.

I regularly considered going back to school for an advanced degree, but it seems to me that in this modern age of advanced technology and declining academic standards, a formal education is less effective and less meaningful than it has been in generations past.

Instead, I focused my attention on understanding how all of the elements I was learning about intersected and informed one another, and developed a holographic framework to better make sense of our cultural trajectory and my place in it.

One day I realized I'd had all the jobs that I wanted, in all of the industries that fueled my passion. I'd produced television, designed video games, consulted for startups, had a brief stint in publishing, even slung cocktails behind a bar.

I'd also seen what worked, and what didn't, as people moved through their lives and careers. I'd paid attention to who was able to achieve success and who seemed to flounder, and I'd seen a series of patterns emerging.

So I decided to turn my attention to helping others experience the same joy and success that I had attained, and put those observations to better use.

November, 2017
www.butterfly-soup.com

CPSIA information can be obtained
at www.ICGtesting.com
Printed in the USA
BVOW08s1720181117
500744BV00006B/10/P